PROMISE OF GREATNESS

PROMISE
OF GREATNESS

THE WAR OF 1914-1918

Edited by George A. Panichas

Foreword by Sir Herbert Read

THE JOHN DAY COMPANY

NEW YORK

Library of Congress Catalogue Card Number: 68–24147

PRINTED IN THE UNITED STATES OF AMERICA
BY AMERICAN BOOK–STRATFORD PRESS, INC.

Foreword

THE CONTRIBUTORS to this volume, most relating their experiences of a war that took place fifty years ago, speak as witnesses or students of an event that has had no parallel in recorded history. Wars there have been since the beginning of human history, and all have been desperate, bloody, and futile. Sometimes they have been redeemed by heroism, by self-sacrifice, and by what, with many qualifications, we may call patriotism.[1] The peculiarity of the First World War was that, as the name we now give it indicates, it was the first *world* war; more than that it was, as Edwin Erich Dwinger indicates in the title of his contribution, the first *civil* war within Europe: a war that apart from preliminary skirmishes by professional troops was fought by hastily trained civilians for reasons that were never clear to them at the time, for causes that have only been obscured or made ambiguous by subsequent historical research. Most of our contributors bear witness to the fact, baffling to the warmongers at home, that no specific hatred was felt on one side for the combatants on the other side of what we called no-man's-land. Among the British soldiers the common name for the Germans opposite them was Jerry, almost a term of affection. Brutalities in the heat of battle did occur; men went berserk, an animal intoxication that comes from the smell of blood and powder, the drumbeat of the guns, and the instinct for self-defense. But such face-to-face encounters took place at relatively long intervals. The normal condition of the soldier on the western front was one of stoical endurance: an endurance of prolonged physical hardships that was perhaps a severer ordeal than any fear of death in combat.

The fear of death, as most of our contributors testify, was not for the majority an obsession or even a persistent worry. Such fear is

---

[1] A word acceptable only in this sense: "Our peasants love their villages. The Romans were ardent patriots, when Rome was a mere township. When it became more powerful, their patriotism was not so keen. A city that was mistress of the world was too vast for the hearts of its citizens. Men are not made to love immensity." (Vauvenargues, *Reflections and Maxims,* trans. by F. G. Stevens [London, 1940].)

dissipated in companionship, and companionship, or camaraderie, came as a revelation to most participants: It was a human relationship and a reality that had not existed in times of peace. It overcame (or ignored) all distinctions of class, rank, or education. We did not call it love; we did not acknowledge its existence; it was sacramental and therefore secret.

If we did not feel fear, we knew instinctively that we were doomed. A few of us might survive—and did survive (as this book testifies). But we had no hope of survival, and that made our destiny tragic, as tragic as the destiny of the heroes of a Greek drama. We were participants in such a pre-Christian unredemptive tragedy: the gods in their malice and jesting being represented by the invisible generals who commanded us; the obscene chorus being the politicians and journalists of a country that was so remote that we British gave it a new name, Blighty. We played out that tragedy to the end, never knowing what the end might be. A future, from 1916 onward, did not exist for us. We learned how to live from day to day, from hour to hour, believing that the only future was death, a future to which we were indifferent.

Simone Weil, in her great essay on the *Iliad*, says: "That men should have death for their future is a denial of nature. As soon as the practice of war has revealed the fact that each moment holds the possibility of death, the mind becomes incapable of moving from one day to the next without passing through the specter of death. Then the consciousness is under tension such as it can only endure for short intervals." The daily sufferance of such violence in war, she concludes, "wipes out every conception of a goal, even all thoughts concerning the goals of war."[2] We thought, on the western front, that we had lost any conception of a goal because (as again almost all the contributors to this volume remark) our generals never confided in us, and we were altogether out of touch with those who directed the war from London or Paris. But perhaps Simone Weil is right: The real reason was a kind of insensibility induced by the ever-present specter of death. At the time we would have been too proud or too stupid to admit such a psychological explanation.

The sense of doom varied in intensity according to the quality of one's experience of war. A field surgeon, such as Sir Geoffrey Keynes, was too busy patching up the mutilated bodies that came down from the trenches in their thousands to have anything but a sense of mercy or of pity. Pity was Wilfred Owen's word; the subject of his poems, he wrote, is war, and the pity of war. "The poetry is in

<hr>

[2] *Intimations of Christianity Among the Ancient Greeks*, trans. by Elisabeth Chase Geissbuhler (London, 1957), p. 41.

the pity." But he admitted there was no consolation in such poetry; pity was irrelevant to the truth about war—all the truthful poet could do was to warn.

And yet, it will be said, many people survived the war without experiencing the tragic emotions I have attributed to the common soldier. If I understand Charles Carrington's contribution rightly, he is of the opinion that it is only "literary men" who "agonize" about war. Certainly we may have been disillusioned by the war, all of us who saw it nakedly, but it is better to follow Horace's advice and not to blab about it. "Honest silence brings a sure reward." That might have been good counsel to give to a Roman hero or even to a Roman coward, but any comparisons from the past (even from Homer, the first and greatest realist of warfare) is invalid for the war that broke out in 1914. It was a war of an unparalleled kind: not only, as we have observed, a civil war on an unparalleled scale, but a genocidal war, waged by each side against women and children no less than against conscripted men. That fact alone made it tragic, in a sense in which even the Trojan War was not tragic. But tragedy, let us admit, is an artifact and always man-made; it is the supreme human effort to redeem life from absurdity.

This book is not a tragedy or written in a tragic spirit: It is a collection of reminiscences and reflections that are the raw material for tragedy. The First World War, in any literary sense, will not be made the subject of a tragedy by any of its survivors, and it is doubtful if such a tragedy will be written for many generations. There have been intimations of an epical treatment of these events (such as David Jones' *In Parenthesis*), but all major forms of art require (in the words of Georges Poulet) a "plenitude which is no longer secured by the operation of a personal memory but by the operation of a general memory which, in one state of consciousness, takes in the life of all humanity."[3] About three centuries are supposed to separate Homer from the war he made the subject of his *Iliad*. According to some of our contemporary prophets, poetry as an art will not survive long. These fragments, therefore, are doubly precious, in that they record the substance of a world tragedy and for a long time, perhaps forever, may have to serve (with similar fragments already published) as a substitute for a work of art that would give universal significance to a unique historical event.

April, 1968

HERBERT READ

---

[3] *Studies in Human Time*, trans. by Elliott Coleman (Baltimore, 1956), p. 30.

Acknowledgments

THIS VOLUME of essays could not have been assembled without the assistance of my colleagues and friends. Thus it gives me pleasure to thank them for the help and the time which they so generously gave to this project in the course of the last two years.

To my colleagues in the Department of English, University of Maryland, College Park, Professors Charles Manning, dean of the College of Arts and Sciences; Morris Freedman, head of the department; Kurt G. Weber; and Raymond Thorberg—I am grateful for their support, which they demonstrated variously and abundantly. I am especially proud to be associated with the University of Maryland—its staff, its administration, and its student body—and I wish to acknowledge for the public record its steadfast interest in and endorsement of my research and teaching.

To Miss Martha Seabrook, of the University of Maryland Library —I want to express appreciation not only for her advice and friendship, but also for her painstaking reading of my Introduction, which, because of her invariably perceptive editing, was saved from stylistic and factual errors. Throughout my tenure in the University of Maryland, I have derived much benefit from her consideration of my work, and she has also shared with me her wide and discerning knowledge of literature, particularly the modern British novel.

To Miss Mary E. Slayton, of the Library of Congress, I want once again to voice my gratitude for her diligence and industry in aiding me in the immense correspondence and secretarial work necessitated by such a big and "international" volume of essays; in typing and retyping many of the manuscripts; and, not least of all, in reading and correcting galley proofs. Her patience and constant and selfless readiness to assist me with these, as well as with other, innumerable chores, can be deservingly cited but can never be fully estimated.

To Mrs. Alda W. Brincefield, Miss Linda L. Koelker, Joseph Lalley, Miss Susan Myerberg, N. Frederick Nash, Andrew Panichas, Mrs. Miriam B. Wood, and Professors Carl Bode, Richard B. Hovey, Lewis A. Lawson, and Charles D. Murphy—I am indebted for their kindnesses. And to Alan Tucker, editor, the John Day Company, I want to give thanks for his belief in this project. From beginning to end he was sensitive to the historical and literary significance of the book, and I gladly salute him.

Finally, words fail me in assessing the collaboration of the distinguished contributors to this volume. It remains for their own essays to testify to their willingness to write for the book and to the enthusiasm with which they responded to its aims. Their own lives and accomplishmens are what have made possible the publication of *Promise of Greatness* as a gift to history.

Contents

SOCIAL-HISTORICAL PERSPECTIVES 377

LITERATURE OF WAR   477

THE GUILT   557

*A map of part of the western front precedes
the essay by Robert Graves.*

Introduction

No ONE who was born and has lived in the twentieth century has been spared from war, from either the reality or the constant thought and threat of war. This century has seen wars fought with ever-increasing ferocity. Perhaps no other war stirs the emotions more or exerts more lasting interest than does World War I—the Great War of 1914–18, the Great War for Civilization. Although a half century has passed since the Armistice of November 11, 1918, not only in the memories of the survivors, those who fought and those who did not fight, but also in the imaginations of those who were not living at the time, the Great War holds a place of importance which grows stronger as the events of the war come gradually to belong to a distance in the past which gives rise to legend and song and poetry, to the tale of war: the mingling of romance and history into which war has merged from the earliest of times.

War as we have experienced it in this century can hardly arouse exaltation. We have come to see the utter devastation and meaninglessness of war, those cruel realities that the bloodstained face of history has taken on. We have had to learn to confront war not as abstraction but as actuality, "the great unequal battle . . . between the forces of terror and the forces of dialogue," as Albert Camus expressed it. War has made us and our age harder and more cynical. Certainly men today refuse to connect the waging of war with the mystique of adventure: the fulfillment of some inborn promise, the matchless opportunity to display a chivalrous temper. It seems that we have learned war's lessons of illusion and disillusion. The rhetoric of war, which we find as deplorable as it is irresponsible, has no place in a world where nuclear annihilation poses the final menace—and the final madness.

Our attitude toward war that is expressed nowadays in such militant and clamorous ways underlines the fact that the twentieth century is no longer young or naïve. Indeed, when we consider some of the immediate responses to the declaration of war in August, 1914, we recognize innocence, the innocence of youth on the threshold of a new age in an old world with which this century began, when as C. E. Montague later wrote in *Disenchantment,* "All the air was ringing with rousing assurances."[1] "The air is better to breathe than it has been for years . . . ," declared (Sir) Walter Raleigh, professor of English literature at Oxford University.[2] In Vienna, Sigmund Freud exclaimed, "All my libido is given to Austro-Hungary."[3] In France one writer expected that the war would be "amusing," another that it would provide the opportunity to "picnic on the grass."[4] And in Germany one thinker asserted that because his nation had discovered the factor of a higher organization, the war would provide the occasion for reorganizing Europe—and, concurrently, for realizing the German dream of the *Kolossal.*[5] Time and history had not yet run out of promises for the generation of 1914–18. The experience of the war harmonized with the language of heroism, as the early years of the war amply demonstrated. These years held golden moments, "the eve of our crowning hour," according to a soldier-poet. Many men who enlisted in that war felt they were fighting not only for age-old concepts but also for the sake of changing the world and shaping a new destiny.

From a vantage point fifty years later we come to realize that the Great War in its early stages was fought not so much to destroy an enemy as to defend and to extend the possibilities of civilization, and precisely that civilization which Henry James envisioned as the way "to find and to make the earth a friendlier, an easier, and especially a more various sojourn."[6] It is on transcendent levels of the abstract and the ideal and the romantic that we first view the waging of this war. Comradeship, splendor, glory, honor, love, sympathy were still to retain those values vital to a humane civilization. The war was seen in 1914 as a conflict "between sisters, between Martha and Mary, the efficient and intolerant against the casual and sympathetic,"[7] between the real and the unreal, the effete

---

1 (New York, 1922) , p. 3.

2 Quoted in Virginia Woolf, "Walter Raleigh," in *Collected Essays,* (London, 1966) , Vol. I, p. 327.

3 Ernest Jones, *The Life and Work of Sigmund Freud,* ed. and abridged by Lionel Trilling and Steven Marcus (New York, 1963 [1961]) , p. 327.

4 See Julien Benda, *The Betrayal of the Intellectuals,* trans. by Richard Aldington with an Introduction by Sir Herbert Read (Boston, 1955 [1928], p. 140.

5 Romain Rolland, *Above The Battle,* trans. by C. K. Ogden (Chicago, 1916) , pp. 111 ff.

6 *Within the Rim* (London, 1918) , p. 90.

7 *The Letters of Charles Sorley,* W. R. Sorley, ed. (Cambridge, England, 1919) , p. 232.

and the vital, the conscious and the unconscious, the *homo contra-humanus* and the *homo humanus*. As such for many of its partici-pants, and for its nonparticipants, too, this war acted as "a great remedy" and "a great experience," a breakthrough at long last from the dreamworld of the nineteenth century. "You won't catch me complaining of any war—much less of a great war like this that we wage on both sides like mystics for a reason beyond reason," Robert Frost wrote in a letter dated September 17, 1914.[8]

Combatants were characterized again and again by an enthusiasm bordering on religious frenzy. For not a few the war at the front was transposed into a religious experience which provided in its own forms a heightening and a lucidity and a freedom, emerging from shared suffering and death, that no human action could approxi-mate. In battle one experienced a "compelling fascination . . . that lies . . . [in] War's power": "Once you have lain in her arms you can admit no other mistress. You may loathe, you may execrate, but you cannot deny her."[9] Likewise, the war served as a baptism into reality, as it were, a tragic, even ecstatic dimension of life that a soldier-priest, Pierre Teilhard de Chardin, who was cited as "an outstanding stretcher-bearer," envisioned as "an urgent invitation to prayer" while one lived "in a forward-looking tension." Only at the front, with "its noble struggles" and "its impassioned quests," in the ever-present shadow of danger, Teilhard de Chardin believed, could one attain a fully conscious state, a new form of soul, "to be healed and made perfect," and experience there, in "the thick of human endeavour, and with no stopping for breath," what he could not experience anywhere else: that sense of exaltation which comes with "fulfilling a function far higher than that of the individual."[10] Charles Hamilton Sorley, despite a "mute and burning rage and annoyance and sulkiness," felt something of the same when he confessed that in battle "one learns to be a servant. The soul is disciplined."[11]

This was far from assuming some merely sentimental attitude or some lingering heroic dream evoked by schoolboy memories of the "plains of windy Troy," which elated Rupert Brooke upon his de-parture for the Dardanelles in late February, 1915. "Will Hero's Tower crumble," he asked, "under the 15″ guns? Will the sea be polyphloisbic and wine-dark and unvintageable? Shall I loot

---

[8] *Selected Letters of Robert Frost*, Lawrance Thompson, ed. (New York, 1964), p. 134.

[9] Guy Chapman, *A Passionate Prodigality* (London, 1965 [1933]), p. 226.

[10] Pierre Teilhard de Chardin, *The Making of a Mind*, trans. by René Hague (New York, 1961), p. 205, and *Hymn of the Universe*, trans. by Simon Bartholomew (New York, 1961), p. 54.

[11] *The Letters of Charles Sorley*, pp. 220, 312.

mosaics from St. Sophia, and Turkish Delight, and carpets? Should we be a Turning Point in History? Oh God!"[12] For many of the fighting men the war was much more than the excitation of the "confident and glorious hopes"—and questions—that stirred in Brooke. And it was much more, surely, than what H. G. Wells described with commanding import when he asserted: "This, the greatest of all wars, is not just another war—it is the last war!"[13] If for some men the war meant the renovation of mankind by the creation of a "great society," as well as "a new map of Europe," when, as a young French novelist wrote to Romain Rolland, "History will tell of us, for we are opening a new era in the world,"[14] for others it signified the ultimate confrontation of the realities which lie far beyond and far deeper than just "a necessity of honour," for which one statesman pleaded, or an opportunity to "travel along the road of human destiny and progress, at the end of which we shall see the patient figure of the Prince of Peace, pointing to the Star of Bethlehem that leads us on to God," as an English journalist averred.[15]

Hence for some of the fighting men the war—"the whole sad man-made complication," as Rainer Maria Rilke termed it—transcending the romantic and idealistic, transcending, too, what some fighting men designated as "a state of primal innocence," the war enabled one to grasp a better concept of the nature of man and of life as a whole. Above all, it disclosed that evil in the world is not rooted merely in oppression but is an intrinsic part of the nature of things. The realities of the condition of man and of life at the front; the nightmare of slaughter and wooden crosses that the Great War became—these were facts that unmasked the demonic character of man who had sinned and fallen. Life at the front was thus the furthest extension of man's essential condition: his weakness and imperfectibility strained to their most extreme limits. "In this war, then, we are fighting for no great *liberation* of mankind," T. E. Hulme wrote from the trenches, "for no great jump upward, but are merely accomplishing a work, which, if the nature of things was ultimately 'good,' would be useless, but which in this actual 'vale of tears' becomes from time to time necessary, merely in order that bad may not get worse."[16]

The war suddenly awakened the 1914 generation from the com-

---

12 Edward Marsh, *Rupert Brooke. A Memoir* (New York, 1926) , p. 163.
13 *The War That Will End War* (New York, 1914) , p. 14.
14 *Above the Battle, op. cit.,* p. 39.
15 Julian Symons, *Horatio Bottomley* (London, 1955) , p. 174.
16 *Further Speculations,* Sam Hynes, ed. (Lincoln, Nebraska, 1962) , p. 184.

parative ease and comfort and orderliness of an older and more stable way of life. Left behind was the leisurely world of European society before 1914—when education was centered in the classics, when cricket and the hunt often meant much more than international affairs, when private life was valued, when writing poetry and exploring the countryside were sources of quiet joy—a world still close to Thomas Hardy's "indispensable conditions of existence [which] are attachment to the soil of one particular spot by generation after generation."[17] Even as it caused incredulity, disarray, anguish, the declaration of war awakened dreams of glorious exploits echoing once more to the roll of drums. Stefan Zweig, reflecting on the reasons why Europe went to war, suggests that it was not because of ideologies or even provocative acts but rather because of a "surplus of force, a tragic consequence of the internal dynamism that had accumulated in those forty years of peace and now sought violent release."[18] Those who had come to manhood under the discipline of the old tradition had suddenly to face the demands of a new age. Indeed, the war was as much an awakening to these demands as it was a military event. And one of the clearest demands after that "monstrous August" was that the war must correspond with the essential character of a civilization which was becoming increasingly industrialized.

The military conduct of the war mirrored a great transition. Dreams of cavalry charges, of open warfare with dashing officers leading not conscripts but professional soldiers into the fray, into a struggle of strength and skill and courage, had to give way, and at a tremendous expense of lives and material, to the grim exigencies of a fighting front thick with barbed wire and gashed by trenches. This was a new war in a new age. It was a total, an absolute, war; it involved many nations and war fronts and was fought with revolutionary tactics and with new weapons of annihilation—airplanes, submarines, tanks, trench bombs, poison gas. In short, modern warfare was to prescribe the methods of wholesale violence. At the same time, disclosing the denial of personality, it was a struggle directed against men as objects. As such, this war was to be a portent of an age progressively sacrificing the personal to the needs of machine-made mass civilization. "As a man as of a knife: does it cut well? Nothing else mattered," D. H. Lawrence wrote in *Women in Love*, which "took its final shape in the midst of the war."[19] His

---

17 "Preface," *Far from the Madding Crowd* (New York, 1960 [1874]) , p. vii.
18 *The World of Yesterday. An Autobiography* (New York, 1943) , p. 197.
19 (New York, Modern Library Edition [1920]) , p. 254; Foreword, p. ix.

words instance the objectivization that war in the modern industrial world has since procured on demand time and time again.

That the Great War was to be the source of many achievements in prose, in poetry, in drama, and in autobiography and memoirs is not surprising. Literature, after all, reflects both the values and the impulses of an age. For the generation of 1914 these impulses were eminently generous. The drabness of mechanical civilization had not yet conditioned men who, even in the cockpit of slaughter and in the darkness of battle, still apprehended the call of beauty, the passage of the seasons, the spirit of place. Just as war had a deeply religious dimension for some of its combatants, so too did it have a deeply poetic dimension when the creative and destructive instincts, imagination and power, strove for expression. Undoubtedly the immediate scenes of fighting, the desolate, defiled, charred, scarred landscape, now beyond description, strange and dead, inhuman, empty—empty of hope and abandoned by God—were not without their communicable, and incommunicable, impressiveness. Men who had lived in Arcadia were now trapped in Armageddon, but the past lingered precariously in their memory. In the tension between terror and memory was born art, which, as André Gide has told us, "if born of constraint, lives by struggle, dies of freedom."

The literature of the war, as written by participants and by survivors both during and after the conflict, invariably reflects a yearning for truth, a struggling search for some deep understanding of war that, never ignoring the passion of the experience, yet attains the detachment necessary to measure it. What we detect so often in the generation and in the literature of 1914–18 is an intensity of awakening to reality and to truth. Many of the combatants recognized as never before the problematic human situation and likewise discovered truth of self. Bodily and mentally, men rose through the experience of war to the experience of self-meaning. Many of the recollections of the war verbalize the process of discovering some truth of self, of life. Thus, for many soldiers, regardless of nation, the Great War as the home of their youth dramatized in extremity what the world included.

If the war meant anguish, it also meant "the infinite pain of self-realization," to use a phrase of William Butler Yeats, who, incidentally, dismissed the war as a "bloody frivolity." In one sense, perhaps, true heroism was to be experienced precisely in such an awakening. There was the growing awareness of the elemental value of dogged hanging on in an interminable conflict of great

military "offensives" and "deadlocks." Reading the reminiscences
of life at the front, we are struck by the fact that soldiers had to
wait so long for things to happen; that determination itself was
tested by a war in which time had come to a desperate standstill.
"There really seems no reason why the Germans and ourselves,"
said French President Raymond Poincaré at the end of the first year,
"should not stand facing one another for all eternity."[20] Indeed, it
was a war in which there was as much a despair of time as there was
of death. Time is associated with an agonizing sense of unreality
often arising from an awareness of an isolated world reduced to
utter devastation and putrefaction. The picture of this world, where
life and death at last became one, represented for some of the
soldiers a nightmarish eternity. At the front, time stopped for
violence to pass, and the alternating periods of violence and of still-
ness, of savage bombardments followed by sudden silence, blended
to render time dimensionless, indistinct. Time, it seems, had also
become the victim of the irreversibility of destruction and death.
And endurance, if anything, had to take its place and the place of
faith.

But the war also meant a more passionate awakening than just
learning how to endure. This was an experiential awareness of men
sharing dangers, undergoing the drudgery of trench warfare, having
the same fears, disappointments, complaints, resentments, irrita-
tions, disgusts, the same hopes and dreams and enthusiasms, fighting
and surviving, or dying, in a world which they alone knew. Endurance, which must inevitably consist in physical and spiritual weari-
ness that defies death and nothingness, was made more achievable
by a confraternity of men in arms and by a sense of identity that
could be grasped only in the most extraordinary of human situa-
tions. This shared identity was not established just on the fact of
youth in sight of chaos or on intense comradeship emerging in a
world from which there was no easy escape. After all, no lines of
discrimination based on class or favor could exist among men
thrown together in a war that imposed on them an equivalent
danger and equivalent conditions of fighting and of dying. When
time had no meaning and when civilized living had been necessarily
reduced in space to the rubble of no-man's-land, men sought their
remaining human identity through communion with one another.
Beyond this identity there could be nothing else that counted.

In one another, it can be said, the soldiers fighting at the front

20 *The Memoirs of Raymond Poincaré,* trans. by Sir George Arthur (London, 1929),
Vol. III, p. 295.

grew to greatness. In a world where everything seemed to be in a state of collapse, ranging from the failures of leadership at home and at the front to the failures of the announced promise of "victory" battles, they looked for something surer than mere promises or the vagaries of faith. And they found this assurance in fellowship with their comrades. Exposed to maximum dangers, the men in the front lines learned to speak a language based on a unity of experience. They had found promise and truth in one another, even as they learned to accept and inspire one another. Not seldom, in fact, soldiers who had been returned to civilian areas for rest and re-cuperation yearned to be sent back to the battlefield. (Recovering from war wounds in England, Siegfried Sassoon felt the "awful attraction" that the war held over his mind, and he was "disquieted by a craving to be back on the Western Front as an independent contemplator."[21]) Their feelings for one another were a mixture of respect and pity, based on an experience of life born and tested and renewed in the heat of conflict. As their accounts demonstrate, these men did not hate utterly. For them the war, much deeper than the fastness of hate, was the passion of its suffering, when in the course of cruel history "I hear, through dead men's drums, the riddled lads/Strewing their bowels from a hill of bones,/Cry Eloi to the guns"[22]—the suffering, that is to say, mitigated by a common human identity and fulfilled in a common judgment: When all are to blame, all are accused.

The many brave acts of the men who fought in this war must not be judged by the traditional criterion of prowess or the old concept of the heroic man of action. This was an altogether new and mech-anized war, ungraced by those inexpressibly strange felicities and nobilities engendered by older wars, even at their most savage heights. The Nietzschean view of men who wage war for the "pleasures of victory and cruelty" so as to be "purified" by their triumphs over the elements and other men and thus become "the archetypes of moral beauty" could hardly be defended or exempli-fied in a war that wrought indiscriminate annihilation. There was nothing beautiful or glorious about this war. Bravery was no longer some spectacular process; when it appeared, it was usually against a dehumanized background of ugliness and disbelief. Essentially a brave act had to be achieved not in some encounter with other men but against the mechanical might of the weapons of destruction produced by a new science and engineering. Bravery, like heroism, was radically transformed in act and meaning in a conflict in which,

---

21 *Siegfried's Journey. 1916–1920* (London, 1945) , pp. 69–70.
22 Dylan Thomas, "My World Is Pyramid," in *Collected Poems. 1934–1952* (London, 1966) , p. 26.

as it transpired, there could be neither complete victory nor complete defeat.

By no means should these observations imply that the soldiers in this war were not as brave as the soldiers in past wars. On the contrary, the men at the front disclosed a bravery all the more astonishing when one considers their inexperience and the awesome surprise that they must have often felt in contending not with other human beings but with the depersonalized ways of modern warfare. The opportunity for individual acts of bravery gave way to the requirements of collective military efforts, now made necessary by a war based on tactics and maneuvers and executed by great armored forces. Under these circumstances bravery became more a matter of holding on tenaciously, even miraculously, against innumerable forms of mechanized power that could bring death swiftly, unexpectedly, at any time, in any place. For many soldiers bravery became a realized inner experience of surmounting fear of the senseless and the pitiless, while at the same time appreciating such things as chance and luck and fate. It became passive, rather than exhibitive. In other words, bravery was something that a soldier had first to search for and discover and exert in himself, and as such it was to be attained anonymously: in the common soldier—the "nobody" as he was sometimes known—struggling to survive a mass killing process which ultimately flouted any distinction between bravery or cowardice.

As the war went on, especially after the Battle of the Somme and the failure of the "Great Advance" in 1916, and as the casualties, the disappointments, and the horrors accumulated, the realization grew that this was a "murder war" now further and further removed from any struggle for civilization, certainly from that phantom civilization which Matthew Arnold once saw as the humanization of man in society. At the front, in the midst of endless barbed-wire entanglements, of advances counted by the inches, of murderous artillery bombardments that led to the disappearance of entire villages and to the creation of cemeteries of mud for men and animals alike, the presage of death became the most immediate fact of life. Military leadership, professionally—and professedly—concerned with what T. E. Lawrence has described as "the whole house of war in its structural aspect, which was strategy, in its arrangements, which were tactics, and the sentiment of its inhabitants, which was psychology,"[23] frequently failed to sustain the soldiers' enthusiasms and trust and, worse, to understand the hell of this war. Errors in judgment, inexcusably inadequate communication,

---

23 *Seven Pillars of Wisdom* (New York, 1966 [1926]) , pp. 162–63.

recklessness, bungling, stubbornness, caprice, irresponsibility, ama-
teurishness, stupidity, especially on the part of the military man-
darins, led to unnecessary death and maiming, as well as to the
cynicism that the fighting men increasingly felt and that in some
French Army units even erupted into mutiny. . . . In "the house
of war" the meed of valor must yet inevitably vie with the spirit's
ruin.

Of all the experiences of war, what remains unwavering in the
survivors' recollections is the omnipresence of death. And it is the
immensity and ugliness and horror of death that haunt their
memories. The scenes in which the soldiers depict death are touched
not so much by mystery or fear as by incomprehensibility. At the
front, death was to come suddenly and with a wide range of devastation. Often it was the unnaturalness of the scenes of death that
seemed so grotesque. Death came with mechanical force, with an
objective relentlessness and an instantaneousness beyond belief.
Though some of the survivors recall separate examples of death
wounds and death experiences, it is more usual for them to depict
scenes of collective death. We are thus reminded of a war in which
entire armies disappeared; death was as massive in its results as it
was incontrovertible in its power. Awesomeness and powerlessness,
consequently, characterize the responses of the fighting men to the
constant danger of death cheaply but efficiently accomplished by
the engines of war.

Oftentimes the survivors recall scenes in which the living and the
dead come together. A soldier seeking refuge and protection in
some pithole finds his only other companion to be a dead soldier.
Or, as he threads his way in the dark, he stumbles against a dying
man. Or, as he is digging, he unearths a khaki-clad corpse covered
by debris in the wake of an earlier artillery bombardment. And too,
there are the memories of mass graves, of burying parties, of smell-
ing corpses being eaten by packs of roaming dogs, of young and
strong bodies deformed beyond recognition. And we are ever aware
of the appalling number of casualties, in a war in which one day
alone could bring death and wounds to many thousands of men and
one year to well over a million. At the front death is the over-
whelming fact. The magnitude of death creates speechless horror;
the thought of death fills immensity. There is hardly a boundary
line between the dead, the dying, and the living. It has been said
that although death destroys a man, the idea of death saves him. But
for the men at the front, death held no comfort of theory by which
one could leap over death as destruction or as salvation. For them
it was the major presence of life: The incessant vision of the
wounded and the dying exceeded pity and prayer alike.

Yet self-pity and sentimentality, offshoots of great spiritual and physical crises, are singularly lacking in these responses. Even where the scenes of death become dread images of mass slaughter, they reflect immense pain felt and a stark recognition of some tremendous force let loose, bringing infinite ruin. Often, therefore, death is seen in the metaphorical guise of madness; it is what could not possibly be real because of its sheer inhumanness, but which in its enormity and momentum moves at last beyond the consciousness of the real and the moral. That life has been violated and blasphemed in man's least sacrosanct moments is what often informs some of the immediate responses to the scenes of death. The victory of a profane spirit becomes an overarching fact. That the word "monstrous" appears repeatedly in the survivors' recollections is not without its significance here: This power that brings death is mechanical and conscienceless; it inflicts death with a kind of measured, passionless intensity. The battle scenes of death reveal the marks of a power that crushes once it strikes, reaping men in swaths.

In the concluding pages of *The Magic Mountain,* Thomas Mann describes the Great War as "The historic thunder-peal, of which we speak with bated breath, [and which] made the foundations of the earth to shake. . . ."[24] Certainly by the time of the Armistice the war had become an experience of the abyss, not only for the fighting men on both sides, but also for entire civilian populations, especially in the immediate areas of the hostilities. This shaking of the foundations of European civilization was brutally evident in every phase of life. After 1918 the values of a settled civilization were gone. The years of the war remained as the chief remembrance of things past, and the future was uncertain. The war had destroyed a sense of security and stability, and 1918 was to become a date signaling the crises of civilization that have marked the rest of the twentieth century. Those who lost their lives lost all their bitterness. But those who survived felt sorrow without end. Recalling the upheavals of the war, Leonard Woolf remarks in *Downhill All the Way:* "In 1914 in the background of one's life and one's mind there was light and hope; by 1918 one had unconsciously accepted a perpetual public menace and darkness and had admitted into the privacy of one's mind or soul an iron fatalistic acquiescence in insecurity and barbarism."[25]

Here Mr. Woolf underlines what can be described as the "deaths in belief" that the generation of 1914–18 suffered. The war was

24 (Harmondsworth, England, 1960 [1924]) , p. 709.
25 (London, 1967) , p. 9.

especially disastrous for idealistic thought, for the innocence of an optimist faith, for the liberal doctrine, for the humanist creed, and for the old ideals of classicism and education. More than anything else, the war had unmasked the most diabolic tendencies and weaknesses of man and his society. Neither the values of a civilization founded on what the English philosopher G. E. Moore termed the "divine voice of a plain common-sense" nor G. Lowes Dickinson's melioristic vision of a world in which man can stretch "feelers into the Dark, laying hold there of stuff, and building mythologies and poems, the palaces of splendid hopes and desires," could possibly withstand the ravages of the war. Modern civilization, in the wake of war, was to become the hostage of a world in which a glorified "authentic present" and a "massive incertitude" (to use here a phrase of Ezra Pounds) agitated to replace the traditions and values that the war had destroyed. Civilization in the period following 1918, then, was a witness both to a dying order and to a world striving to be reborn. But the possibility of resurrection in a world defiled beyond recognition was not without its frightening limitations: "The post-war generation had to live," one writer lamented, "and the war-generation had nothing to give them to live by."[26]

There are always those, of course, who, like Conrad Aiken in *The Soldier,* suggest that "The history of war/is the history of mankind":[27] who suggest that war in the historical process is ultimately a dynamic, cleansing, and creative experience which helps to teach nations and humanity self-knowledge and to release new energy. But surely the Great War was to destroy such a myth! After the Armistice nothing could be more painfully obvious than the absurdity of the promises of war. For what remained—had to remain—was the physical and spiritual shattering that this war had brought to European civilization, not the least of which were the staggering statistics of nearly 9,000,000 men in uniform killed and more than 21,000,000 wounded. Figures by themselves undoubtedly cannot relate a tragedy. Nor indeed can mere descriptions of a holocaust convey its full meaning. The outer crisis of this war—the death of man by man, the destruction, the absurdity, the defilement—was inevitably transcribed into an inner crisis of mind and soul: the alienation, the meaninglessness, the cynicism, the hate, the despair, the confusion, the suspicion, the fear, the doubt that possess modern man even in the midst of his triumphs in science and technology. The legacy of the Great War, as its survivors' reminiscences reveal

---

26 J. Middleton Murry, *Looking Before and After* (London, 1948) , p. 155.
27 (Norfolk, Connecticut, 1944) , p. 16.

and as history attests, was the death of man in flesh and in spirit. Perhaps this is the one truth that can be discovered in the midst of struggle and destiny in those years of conflict.

When the war ended, a feeling of futility set in—a realization that, in the end, little had been gained, much had been lost. This sense of futility is communicated by the survivors over and over again: It haunts their memories and stamps their apprehension of the emptiness of life. A broken promise and a broken world were the most direct results of the war. The war dramatized disorder and divisions and catastrophes. Beyond these tangible manifestations of an annihilative spirit, it also led to a deadening process in the hearts of men. Civilized living, it can be asserted, is nourished by a sense of discrimination, which war blunts and gradually displaces. "Pathos, piety, courage—they exist, but are identical, and so is filth. Everything exists, nothing has value."[28] Thus E. M. Forster sums up the senselessness of existence, and no words could better capture what the Great War finally legislated. More than anything else, in the collapse of the discriminating, civilizing faculty, the war revealed that barbarism is a force which constantly threatens civilization, that civilization itself must occupy a tenuous position in a world in which supreme acts of might instance not only the relative worth of life but its worthlessness as well. For the survivors the war was to produce a clearer and more terrifying recognition of the finite conditions of man's existence.

Barbarism was not confined to the fronts. Nor was it merely resorted to and executed in the service of force and slaughter. Barbarism is as much a dehumanizing process as it is a brutal action or reaction; its eruptions and effects are to be measured in terms not of one area of antagonisms but of a total human situation. If barbarism, then, quickens in the midst of the cannonade and the battle cries of the killing instinct—if, that is, it is a special condition, even requirement, of what happens in warfare—it is also something that embraces what can be called the public life, or the everyday life distant from the war front. During the Great War civilian populations could hardly escape the impact of the war either physically or spiritually. The barbarism of the war was thus extended to include those men and women not immediately involved. Perhaps one of the most far-reaching, brutalizing effects of the war was the bringing to the surface of a crisis of trust between participant and nonparticipant, a breakdown of communication between them. One of the soldiers in Henri Barbusse's *Under Fire,* returning to

---

28 *A Passage to India* (London, 1953 [1924]) , p. 156.

the front after two months' sick leave, brings out this lack of communication when he cries: " 'I'm fed up—*that's* what I am! The people back there, I'm sick of them—they make me spew, and you can tell 'em so!' "[29] It was in the very nature and irrationality of the war, thus, to make more difficult the possibility of authentic dialogue between those who were fighting and those not fighting. (G. E. Moore, for example, admitted that he never felt anything about the war at all. To him it made no difference: "None. Why should it?" he snapped to Lytton Strachey.) [30]

The barbarism of the war at the front, hence, was not without its counterpart in the public life that managed to go on in the apparent safety behind the lines. And among the civilian populations the Great War brought out some of the least desirable qualities and responses. Writing from London in October, 1917, D. H. Lawrence bitterly complained that "People are not people any more: they are factors, really ghastly, like lemures, evil spirits of the dead."[31] For Lawrence the war signified "destruction and dying and corruption," "so much hate . . . and disintegration," when "massive creeping hell is let loose." Lawrence did not serve in the war, but his visionary insights into the condition of the men and women who lived during the war years have a special significance, insofar as they help convey the spirit of the barbarism that possessed whole populations. Its manifestations were numerous: "Talkers," "word makers of war," statesmen, and profiteers (war's "vested interests bawling patriotically and making money"[32]) united to oil the propaganda machines and to inflame public opinion with atrocity stories and spy scares. Religious leaders, preaching "the Gospel of the Spiked Helmet" and exhorting "Christ-loving soldiers," claimed that the choice had to be made between "the nailed hand" and "the mailed fist." Young women presented white feathers to men who for one reason or another were not serving in the armed forces. And some parents publicly displayed their sons' military medals—and their sons—with a sense of pride tantamount to the most glossy barbarism.

Nothing ever remains sacred in war, which embodies disorder and affliction *ne plus ultra*. It generates habits of violence. It muddles human consciousness. It accentuates, above all, the ceaseless struggle between barbarism and its proper opposite, civilization.

---

[29] Trans. by Fitzwater Wray (New York, 1917) , p. 112.

[30] Michael Holroyd, *Lytton Strachey. A Critical Biography* (New York, 1968) . Vol. II, p. 148.

[31] *The Collected Letters of D. H. Lawrence,* Harry T. Moore, ed. (New York, 1962) , Vol. I, p. 528.

[32] Desmond MacCarthy, *Memories* (New York, 1953) , p. 141.

The Great War proved that the barbaric element, far from having been refined out of existence, in a world of immense technological progress, remains a perpetual threat. Europe in the course of the war saw the deterioration of rational, civilizing values, particularly the value of life, not only in the destruction and death on the war fronts, but also in the widespread demoralization of life distant from the front. The Great War increasingly absorbed the energies of soldier and civilian alike. No one was to be immune from the barbarism that war provokes or blameless in the savageries committed against civilized life and thought. Tested and pressured by a war augmented by the inexorable powers of the newly evolved, and evolving, technique and apparatus of an industrial society, the very structure and consciousness of Europe crumbled. For European civilization, therefore, the Great War meant both death and world-weariness: death for the soldier, world-weariness for the civilian. It compelled the depersonalization of life, as well as its sacrifice to a mechanized materialism abrogating all human value. "The terrible, terrible war," to cite Lawrence once more, "made so fearful because in every country practically every man lost his head, and lost his own centrality, his own manly isolation in his own integrity, which alone keeps life real."[33]

The war, transforming men, transformed Europe. More than anything else, it shattered man's inner life by destroying faith in himself and in his own worth. By 1918 the soul had been humiliated. With the end of the war European man was to be acutely aware of the deceptiveness of his prewar belief, fashioned in more spacious, less thought-tormented days, that his refinement and essential civilization had at last, in this century and in this world, defeated barbarism. Immunity from the barbarism of the subhuman and the antihuman was to be one of modern man's serious deaths in belief. For the "European spirit" and the "European mind" the Great War showed civilization disintegrating—that "rhythm of disintegration," as Arnold Toynbee calls it[34]—which was equated with "breakdown," "collapse," "paralysis." The war consituted a multiple barbarism of might, the fundamental, most exhaustive consequence of modern man's capacities and progress, his technical resources, his industries—his audacity. Europe submitted to this might, to this technique, and the disaster was incalculable: It had to be appraised on a scale of conflict and consequence and change manifoldly greater than in any previous conflict, involving not localized objectives and limited fighting numbers and fronts, but

---

[33] *Kangaroo* (Harmondsworth, England, 1960 [1923]) , p. 236.
[34] *A Study of History,* abridged by D. C. Somervell (New York, 1946) , Chap. XXI.

a total society, in which the whole was at war with its parts. Superseding the "old geometry of history" and "the old mechanics of power," the war showed that "melodic history" was no longer possible.[35] The meaning of history, like the spirit and mind of Europe, could hardly remain the same after the events of 1914–18.

"We later civilizations . . . we too now know that we are mortal," Paul Valéry wrote in the *Athenaeum* in 1919, his famous words arising from the depths of the ruins and the anguish of the Great War.[36] The passage from war to peace, he believed, was darker and more dangerous than the passage from peace to war. "'Peace," he continued, "is perhaps that state of things in which the natural hostility between men is manifested in creation, rather than destruction as in war."[37] Valéry's remarks stress the mortality of European civilization and of the European psyche that the war had evinced. The problems of the "great peace" after the military crisis was over were to agonize the conscience of Europe throughout the years before the next war. The war itself was an omen of the peace that ensued: the exhaustion of a civilization in spirit and in mind, as much as in body.

Sir Herbert Read notes that the Great War has not yet been, nor in all probability will be, the subject of a tragedy or of a great epic work by any of its survivors: Rather, the war's tragic meaning will have to be discovered, and its total human drama rendered, in the various reminiscences and reflections that have been appearing since 1914. Yet if the Great War, with the passage of half a century, has not lent itself to tragic or epic expression, it has, in the divers literary forms of the fragments that have been written, disclosed what is just as imperishable and just as sacred a manifestation of the creative spirit: prophetic vision. This vision arises from a special knowledge, in itself a result of experiencing some historical happening in civilization at its midnight hour, and communicates with a sense of urgency a special revelation, that burden of vision which a Hebrew prophet depicted as his responsibility to "Write the vision and make it plain, upon tables, that he may run that readeth it."[38] No less than other celebrated writers in the great prophetic tradition which extends back to the ancient Hebrews, the survivors of the Great War often "see" and "speak" in their writings with a prophetic power that reveals hidden truths. And like great prophets

---

35 Paul Valéry, *History and Politics,* trans. by Denise Folliot and Jackson Mathews (New York, 1962) , pp. 115, 116.
36 *Ibid.,* as reprinted, p. 23.
37 *Ibid.,* p. 29.
38 Habakkuk 2:2.

who see more than they ought to see, they speak directly from the inner fact of things with an immediacy of experience and concern endowing their vision with a truth no less significant or imperative than that with which the ancient prophet demanded of his people, "Hear this word."

Prophetic literature is a "literature of crisis." It emerges in the midst of breakdown. It is addressed to men who do not know, who do not understand. It decries the violation of the dignity of life. It protests against human debasement. It speaks not only of what is happening or has happened, but also of what can happen. The prophetic voice has no finality in the historical setting in which suffering is uncircumscribed. With the pain of experience and with a compassion and a pathos that endure, the prophet's words register a special awareness, beyond experience itself—even beyond man himself. Prophets, Paul Tillich suggests, "are like the refined instruments which register the shaking of the earth on far-removed sections of its surface."[39] These words crystallize some of the essential qualities and functions of the writings of those who fought in the Great War. For these writings summon us to take part in a time of crisis of a guilt-ridden epoch, to recognize a historical situation, and to fathom its disaster as it is re-created and reflected in words— in the vision—that echo the Hebrew prophet's own lament: "The harvest is past, the summer is ended, and we are not saved."[40] The prophetic spirit, Martin Buber maintains, "instils the vision in the people for all time to come. It lives within the people from then on as a longing to realize a truth."[41] Approached from this view, the literature of war becomes prophecy. Such literature, we can well agree with Sir Herbert, contains "the raw material for tragedy," "the substance of a world tragedy"; but it remains for prophecy to give to it universal significance.

Far from simplifying or sentimentalizing the problem of war, as Douglas Jerrold feared,[42] these writings are prophetic in their warnings. They are quintessentially part of the historical process and witness to "the rebelliousness of the hour" rather than to "the struggle for revelation." Once the war had ended, Rilke remarked, "the world passed out of the hands of God into the hands of men." In an age that has been increasingly concerned with the problematic relation between man and man, not between man and God, it is to

39 *The Shaking of the Foundations* (New York, 1948), p. 7.
40 Jeremiah 8:20.
41 *Pointing the Way: Collected Essays,* trans. by Maurice S. Friedman (New York, 1956), p. 190.
42 See his *The Lie About the War* (Criterion Miscellany, no. 9; London, 1930).

this truth that the war writers turn our attention. The war writer as prophet unveils the spirit of an age in which man, cut off from God and the old value system, is also cut off from other men. The war itself epitomized this schism. The soldier-prophet registers its pain and terror. Indeed, the experience and the forces of terror in this century are announced, are prophesied, in the writings that came out of 1914–18. An event like Virginia Woolf's suicide in 1941 can be connected with the terror, the fanaticism, the violence, which the Great War unleashed. Her suicide note summarizes the terror that appeared with such "unparalleled" savagery in 1914 and was to continue into World War II. Besides, it shows how defenseless a private life, and civilization with it, is in the presence of fear and force, "the last arguments" which, Clive Bell says in *Civilization*,[43] the Great War confirmed. "I feel certain [Mrs. Woolf wrote] that I am going mad again. I feel we can't go through another of those horrible times. And I shan't recover this time. I hear voices and cannot concentrate on my work. I have fought against it, but I cannot fight any longer."[44]

Military despotism, the herd instinct, barbarism—the Great War signaled the entry of these forces of terror into modern life, as the wheels of the universe seemed to roll backward. When the Belgian city of Louvain, with its great library, its art treasures, its famous public buildings, was burned and devastated and its civilian population mercilessly slaughtered in the early days of the war, it was made clear that in a modern "murder war" nothing is preservable, least of all the amenities and sanctities of civilization. From the very beginning of the conflict, the pleas of a Hermann Hesse, in Berne, to artists and thinkers not to be engulfed by the war spirit—*"O Freunde, nicht diese Töne!"*[45]—or the counsel of a Romain Rolland, in Geneva, to remain *"au-dessus de la mêlée,"* were destined by and large to be ignored or to be received as the foolish ideas of "pacifists" and "defeatists." Any expectation of discovering after 1914 "the moral equivalent of war" became redundant. As the war dragged on year in and year out, so did all hope and faith vanish. In the resultant conditions of life, the boredom and the dreariness at the front and away from the front, 1914–18 may be seen as years that lie, in Barbara Tuchman's words, "like a band of scorched earth dividing that time from ours."[46] There died in those lost years— *lost,* for they were years wrenched from the body of life—the hopes

43 Middlesex, England, 1947 [1928], p. 137.
44 Quoted in James Hafley, *The Glass Roof* (Berkeley, 1954), pp. 6–7.
45 *Above the Battle, op. cit.* p. 157.
46 *The Proud Tower* (New York, 1966), p. xiii.

for civilization that life in itself enjoins. This war served as a pro-
logue to an age—particularly to that modern spirit of discontent and
of an endless groping for meaning, for values that the conflict had
all along proved valueless.

As some of the survivors stress, perhaps the greatest casualty of the
war was the collapse of the established values of a social order, of
European civilization extending back to the French Revolution.
Although it had survived the conflagrations of 1830, 1848, and 1870,
this civilization was unequal to the struggle posed by the Great War.
It was unequal to this struggle not because the struggle was no
longer considered necessary or right but because civilization was
unready for the radical nature of a time when history was being
emptied of its past. The Great War degraded the civilizing reti-
cences, whether in the methods and weapons of modern warfare
or in the cause and manner of death. What the survivors often decry
in their writings is the obscenity of the war and, in turn, the obscenity of the "modern mind." On the front lines, as well as at the home,
among statesmen, priests, generals, among soldiers, their parents,
their wives—allies and enemies alike—everyone had submitted to
the obscene process of the war, to that "modern mind" that, out-
distancing itself in its inventions and capacity for invention, had
depraved itself. A war that for many started somehow with a vague
dream of a better world gradually brought the realization that civilization was reverting to the obscenities of life at its most primitive
level. That this shock was overpowering and even impossible to
fathom becomes the burden of the message of the literature of the
Great War and the source of its prophecy.

Many writers depict the Great War as a tragedy in the history of
European civilization. Certainly when the period of this "war-
disease" is examined; when the war's barbarism, both "scientific"
and "systematic," is seen in all its pain and horror; when European
society was reduced to a collective state of destruction or one of
awaiting destruction; when the spirit of the time was no more than
a "hymn to hate," with the voices of reason and compassion giving
way to those of violence—"Have no fear, our force will slay theirs,"
the French philosopher Henri Bergson asserted,[47] and his words
summed up the sentiments on both sides, as even intellectuals and
academicians affirmed that force contains the only solutions—it is
not difficult to detect the tragic ramifications of this war: the calam-
ity, the anguish, the despair, the oppressiveness, the pathos, the
fatefulness which are the constants of all tragedy, classical and

---

47 *The Meaning of the War* (London, 1915) , p. 47.

modern. Characterized by ugliness, cynicism, insensitivity, scorn, criminality, it was tragedy that was mean-spirited, without the beauty, without the wisdom, without the nobility and humanism that redeem tragedy and man. In the tragedy of this war, man's puniness was laid bare with devastating contempt: Man was nothing, degraded as he was to instrumentality by a obscene mechanical process. In a word, the tragedy of the Great War was a modern tragedy of obscenity, when neither man's understanding nor his virtues could resemble or equal those endemic to the ascendant rhythm of ancient tragedy. Such a tragedy could hardly conclude except on the humiliating note of insult and sneer, as the spectacle of the postwar period, right up to 1939, iterated with multiplying examples.

By no means should these remarks imply that the generation of 1914–18 was unequal to or incapable of tragedy. Their writings on the war show only too clearly a grasp of the tragic elements that no survivor of World War II has yet to disclose. From every standpoint the generation that fought in the Great War was a generation made for suffering and heroism in a "war against war." That they were an unsuspicious generation with a passion for idealism and justice and freedom; that they were responsive to "cause" and "principle" and "duty"; that they were as proud and self-confident as they were romantic and naïve; that they were a generation that believed in creative reason, in progress, in civilization, and hence in man's destiny are qualities that the men of 1914 reveal without conscious effort. But if this generation was worthy of heroic attitudes and gestures that still looked back to early times, they were not ready for the changes that affected tragic experience in the modern world. For millions of men the experience of the war was tragic in its physical and mental suffering; in its exposure of the inchoate evil and the chaos existent in the visible world; in its desperation and dilemma, as well as in its hopelessness. But although the phenomenal experience of the war was for many men tragic, the vision implicit in tragedy was not. The mechanical nature of modern warfare had neutralized not only men, but also values. Life had been terribly cheapened; suffering itself had been devalued. The ultimate meaning of the war had been translated into something soulless, into a state that gravitated not to a higher recognition of human value but to meaninglessness.

The war finally constituted an unelevated tragedy, lifted to no noble scale or design, and thus holding no visionary, no revivifying, meaning for man and his world. In place of magnanimity, which is intrinsic to the experience of tragedy with its "divine worth of tones and tears," the war ordained a squalid human destiny, one of